Cast Iron Cookbook

CAST IRON
Cookbook

The Ultimate Guide to Cast Iron Cooking

Julia Grady

DYLANNA**PRESS**

Contents

1
Introduction

THE CAST-IRON SKILLET is an icon of American cooking and has been used for centuries by cooks who understand its many advantages. You may have memories of your grandparents cooking meals in cast iron pans. In fact, since cast iron will last for generations, you may have those very same pans in your kitchen today!

Out of all the different types of cookware in my kitchen, the ones I like best are made of cast iron. Perhaps it's due to nostalgia, but more likely it's because they are among the most versatile pans around and never fail to turn out the most delicious dishes.

Many people are unsure about cast iron cookware and shy away from using it based on fears about it being tricky to cook with or hard to care for. If this is you, then you've come to the right place! This book will guide you through and tell you everything you need to know about cast iron cooking from choosing the right pans, to seasoning them properly, to how to properly clean and store them.

In addition to learning the basics of cast iron cooking, the book also includes an abundance of delicious recipes that are specially suited to the benefits of cast iron. From perfectly cooked bacon and pancakes on the griddle to seared steaks and crispy fried chicken to mouthwatering desserts, *The Cast Iron Cookbook: The Ultimate Guide to Cast Iron Cooking* has you covered.

Let's get cooking!

Benefits of Cast Iron Cooking

Cast iron pans are extremely durable and versatile—no other type of pan material even comes close. This is cookware that is built to last and you would have to work very hard to ruin it completely. In fact, cast iron cookware typically becomes better with age, so count yourself lucky if you happen upon one at a yard sale or flea market.

One of the main benefits of cast iron is its extremely high heat capacity, which means that it can be heated to high levels and once it is heated it will stay hot. This makes it the perfect type of pan for searing meat and frying chicken, or for stir fries. However, cast iron can be prone to uneven heating and will form hot spots while other areas of the pan remain cooler. To avoid this, make sure to allow the pan to preheat on the burner for about 10 minutes, turning it occasionally for even heat distribution. An alternative method for preheating the pan is to place it in a hot oven for 15 to 20 minutes, but be careful when removing as the handle will be extremely hot.

Another feature of cast iron is its high emissivity, or its ability to give off a high level of heat energy. This means that not only the surface of the food is being cooked, but also deep inside and in the higher layers as well. For this reason, it is excellent for roasting meats and vegetables.

Cast iron is oven safe which means that you can use one pan for both braising and baking. Its hot surface will make for crisp pie crusts and golden brown cornbread. Finally, a well-seasoned cast iron pan will provide a smooth, non-stick surface for cooking without the toxic chemicals associated with other nonstick coatings.

Drawbacks of Cast Iron

Of course, cast iron is not without its drawbacks. First off, it is heavy, like extremely heavy. In fact, a large skillet or Dutch oven can weigh up to 20 pounds! Second, care must be taken to properly season the pan. While not difficult, it does take time to get a new cast iron pan seasoned to the point of it being truly nonstick. Another issue is rust. Cast iron must be cleaned and dried soon after using. Prolonged exposure to moisture, such as allowing the pan to drip dry in the sink will invite rust spots. Luckily, if this happens they can be removed fairly easily. A final thing to remember about cast iron is that cooking acidic foods in these types of pans will cause some of the iron to leach out into the food, potentially altering its taste. For this reason cast iron is not the best choice for cooking things such as a long-simmering tomato-based sauce.

Types of Pans

Cast iron cookware is available in a variety of sizes and styles. Here is a rundown of the basic types.

- **Skillets.** Cast-iron skillets are probably the most popular type of pan and every kitchen should have a 10-inch skillet. There are other sizes available, from a small 6-inch pan up to a very large (and heavy!) 17-inch skillet.
- **Griddles.** Griddle pans have a smooth surface, shallow sides, and come in a variety of shapes. These are perfect for cooking up a batch of pancakes.

- **Frying pans.** These types of pans have deeper sides than skillets so that oil and grease does not splash out of the pan when frying.
- **Grilling pans.** Grill pans have a ribbed surface and are used for grilling foods on the stovetop. The grooves hold the drippings and will give food sear marks just like an outside grill.
- **Dutch ovens.** This is another absolutely essential pot to have in your kitchen. These are deep-sided pots with lids that can be used both on the stovetop and in the oven. Some Dutch ovens have an enamel or porcelain coating over the cast iron. These are versatile pots that you will use again and again.
- **Woks.** These types of pans are fantastic for cooking stir fries as well as for deep frying and even for making soups in. Woks have a curved shape and deep sides.
- **Muffin pans and other bakeware.** Cast iron is a great choice for baking because of its heat retention properties. It will help you turn out perfect muffins, pies, and breads every time.

Purchasing Cast Iron Pans

It is possible to find high-quality vintage cast iron pans at yard sales or on eBay. Look for brands such as Wagner and Griswold. If you find one of these, you would be well advised to snap it up before someone else does. These pans were made before the production process changed in the mid-1950s. Before that time, the surface of cast iron pans were polished to a smooth, satiny finish. In today's pans, the final polishing step is typically left out and the surface has a grainier, slightly bumpy surface.

Bare vs. Enamel
Cast iron cookware is available both bare and enamel coated. Uncoated cast iron is less expensive than enameled and has to be seasoned before using to become nonstick. The advantage of enamel-coated pans is that the surface is nonstick without seasoning and it is also rust resistant. Dutch ovens are often purchased with an enamel coating and these are safe for use in both the oven and the stovetop. Some other advantages of enamel-coated cast iron include:
- **Easy to clean.** Enameled cast iron is easy to clean up due to the smooth, glass-like surface that food does not stick to. In addition, many types are dishwasher safe.
- **Color choice.** Unlike bare cast iron, enameled cast iron is available in a wide variety of colors.
- **Safe for glass stove tops.** The enamel coating will not scratch or harm glass stove tops.

Unseasoned vs. Pre-Seasoned

Most new pans that are purchased today will come pre-seasoned. This is advantageous because it will save you a lot of time in getting your pan to be truly nonstick. However, even if you purchase a pre-seasoned pan it is still recommended that you season it yourself for a more durable finish.

Some people prefer to buy unseasoned pans so that they can season them in the way they prefer. While more time-consuming it can lead to excellent results.

Seasoning Your Cast Iron Pans

In order for you to use your pans and create a smooth, nonstick surface for cooking you are going to need to first season your cast iron pans. This is because the surface of an iron pan is filled with tiny, microscopic holes and cracks that need to be filled in to make a smooth surface for cooking. This is where oil, or fat, comes in. The oil, when heated, will polymerize, and form a solid, almost plastic-like substance that adheres to and coats the pan. The more times the pan is coated and seasoned with oil, the thicker and better this nonstick coating will be.

Most new pans come pre-seasoned so much of the hard work has already been done for you and you can get cooking almost immediately. That being said, you should still season your new pan when you get it before cooking your first recipe. The seasoning process is really quite simple. First clean your pan with soap and water to remove any dirt and then dry it thoroughly. Then, rub the surface of the pan with oil using a paper towel. Good types of oil to use include vegetable, canola, or corn oil.

Now, put your pan into a preheated 450 degree F oven. Leave it in there for 30 minutes. Remove from oven and allow it to cool. Repeat two or three times before using your pan for the first time.

After your initial seasoning, you should re-season your pan often. To do this, dry your pan after cleaning and place on burner. Add about a quarter-size dollop of oil to the pan. Rub oil into the pan's surface using a paper towel. Heat until pan is smoking , remove from heat, and let cool.

The more you use your pan, the better the seasoning will be. You can expect it to take a couple of weeks of daily use before your pan is really nonstick enough to cook eggs in without sticking. If you don't use your pan that often then it will take quite a bit longer.

Caring for Cast Iron

You may have heard that you cannot clean your cast iron pans with soap because it will damage the seasoning of the pan. However, in a well-seasoned pan the oil should have bonded to the surface of the metal and washing, or even lightly scrubbing with the scrubby side of a sponge, with soap and water should not affect the seasoning of the pan. However, you do not want to leave a cast iron pan soaking in the sink for too long. It should be washed and then dried as soon as possible.

After each use, when the pan is clean and dry place it on a burner and heat it until it starts to smoke. Remove from heat and then, using a paper towel dipped in oil, rub the pan down. Allow to cool to room temperature before storing.

The seasoning layer in a cast iron pan is really quite durable because it is not just stuck to the surface of the pan but is actually chemically bonded to the cast iron metal. This means that you don't have to be overly concerned about scratching it and it is fine to use metal spatulas and other utensils.

The most important thing about caring for you cast iron pan is not letting it stay wet. As soon as you are finished cleaning it, make sure to dry it completely. A paper towel is often best for this purpose. Even a small amount of water left in the pan can cause a rust spot. If a rust spot does develop, don't panic. You will just need to scrub it away and then re-season the pan.

With the proper care your cast iron pan should last a lifetime.

Tips and Tricks for Cooking with Cast Iron

Acidic foods can react with the metal of the pan and leech into your food. Therefore, cast iron pans should not be your choice when cooking things like marinara sauce or other long-simmering tomato-based or wine-based sauces.

Use the right size burner for your pan. Iron does not conduct heat very well, and this is both an advantage and a disadvantage in a cast iron pan. On the positive side, this is why the pan will stay hot once heated for a long period of time. On the down side, it means if you put a large 12-inch skillet on a small burner the outer edges of the pan are not going to get hot. Cook on your largest burner when using cast iron.

Use a handle cover to protect your hands. The handle of a cast iron pan gets very hot so it is a good idea to use a handle mitt to shield your hands from getting burned. Alternatively, look for pans with wooden or other types of nonconductive handle material.

Avoid using plastic utensils. It is preferable to use wooden or metal tools as much as possible. Since the cast iron heats to a high temperature, a plastic spatula may melt and leave behind toxic residue.

Cast iron can be used for cooking outside on a campfire. A Dutch oven or other type of cast iron pan is great to take on camping trips and can be used right on top of the coals or fire.

Store in a dry place free of moisture. If you are going to store pans on top of one another, place a paper towel or soft cloth between them to prevent scratching.

2
Breakfast Dishes

TEXAS SKILLET BREAKFAST WITH STEAK, POTATO, AND EGGS

....

This hearty breakfast will satisfy you well through lunch.

Servings: 3

....

1 tablespoon olive oil

1 tablespoon butter

10 ounces sirloin steak, diced

3 small russet potatoes, diced

1/2 yellow onion, diced

4 eggs, whisked

Salt and freshly ground black pepper, to taste

....

1.   In a large skillet, heat olive oil and butter over medium-high heat. Add steak in single layer, season with salt and pepper, and cook until steak is browned, stirring occasionally, about 3-4 minutes. Remove from pan and set aside.

2.   Add potatoes to same pan, season with salt and pepper, and cook, stirring occasionally, until potatoes are lightly golden browned, about 5 minutes.

3.   Add onion, stir, and continue to cook until potatoes are tender and onion has softened, about 5 minutes.

4.   Add steak back into pan and stir to combine. Remove mixture from pan and divide between serving plates.

5.   Pour whisked eggs into still hot pan, and scrambled until eggs are just set. Divide equally among plates. Season with additional salt and pepper, if desired.

ZUCCHINI, RED PEPPER, AND SWEET POTATO FRITTATA

If you haven't tried making a frittata before, then you're going to love how easy it is to whip up a complete breakfast or light dinner. Similar to an omelet, but without the flip. You can use just about anything in your frittata, but this combination is colorful and delicious.

Servings: 4

2 teaspoons oil

8 large eggs

1 medium sweet potato, peeled and sliced

1 large zucchini, sliced into thin rounds

1 red pepper, sliced thin

1 tablespoon fresh parsley, chopped

Salt and pepper to taste

1.   Heat oil in skillet over medium-high heat. Add sweet potato and cook until tender, 7-8 minutes.

2.   Add zucchini and red pepper and continue cooking for another 4-5 minutes.

3.   Crack eggs into bowl and whisk until eggs are well blended and frothy.

4.   Pour eggs into pan with vegetable mixture. Season with salt and pepper.

5.   Turn heat down to low and cook until eggs are just set, 8-10 minutes. Eggs will still be loose on top.

6.   Remove pan from heat and place under hot broiler until frittata is golden brown on top.

7.   Sprinkle with fresh parsley for garnish and serve.

PEPPERONI AND SPINACH EGG FRITTATA

Cast iron is excellent for making frittatas and this combination is delicious.

Servings: 2-3

5 eggs

1 teaspoon basil

1/4 teaspoon freshly ground black pepper

Pinch of salt

1/2 cup mozzarella cheese, shredded

1/2 cup chopped spinach

1/4 cup sliced pepperoni

1/4 cup grated Parmesan cheese

2 tablespoons olive oil

1 medium yellow onion, diced

1/2 red bell pepper, diced

1 clove garlic, minced

1.   In a bowl, whisk together eggs, basil, black pepper, and salt. Add in mozzarella cheese, spinach, pepperoni, and Parmesan cheese.

2.   Heat oil in medium-size skillet over medium-high heat. Add onion and bell pepper and sauté for 4-5 minutes, until onion turns translucent and begins to soften. Add garlic and sauté for another minute.

3.   Pour egg mixture into skillet and stir to combine. Lower heat to low and cook until eggs are set on bottom and edges are beginning to set, about 5 minutes.

4.   Remove skillet from burner and place in preheated broiler for 4-5 minutes or until frittata is set on top and beginning to turn light golden brown. Serve hot.

DUTCH APPLE PANCAKE

Worthy of a special breakfast.

Servings: 6

4 eggs

1/2 cup all-purpose flour

1/2 teaspoon baking powder

1/4 cup sugar

1/2 teaspoon salt

1 cup milk

1 teaspoon vanilla extract

2 tablespoons butter, melted

1 teaspoon nutmeg, divided

1/2 cup white sugar, divided

1 teaspoon cinnamon

1/4 cup butter

1 large apple, peeled, cored, and sliced

1.　　In a mixing bowl, stir together eggs, flour, baking powder, sugar, and salt. Slowly add in milk. Add vanilla, melted butter and nutmeg. Refrigerate batter for at least 30 minutes.

2.　　Preheat oven to 425 degrees F.

3.　　In a small bowl, mix together 1/4 cup sugar, 1/2 teaspoon nutmeg, and cinnamon.

4.　　In a 10-inch cast iron skillet, melt butter over medium heat. Sprinkle in sugar mixture. Layer apple slices into skillet and sprinkle with remaining sugar. Continue to cook over medium heat for several minutes.

5.　　Pour batter over apples and bake in oven for 20-25 minutes.

ZUCCHINI AND RED PEPPER SHAKSHUKA

Shakshuka means eggs poached in a spicy tomato and onion sauce. This one-pan meal is perfect for breakfast or dinner.

Servings: 4

3 tablespoons olive oil

3 cloves garlic, minced

1 large yellow onion, sliced thin

1 large zucchini, cut into bite-size chunks

2 red peppers, diced

1 cup tomato sauce

2 bay leaves

1 teaspoon crushed red pepper

½ cup fresh cilantro, chopped

Himalayan salt and freshly ground black pepper to taste

8 large eggs

1.   Heat olive oil in large skillet over medium-high heat. Add garlic and onions and sauté for 3-4 minutes until onions soften and turn translucent.

2.   Lower heat to medium and add zucchini and peppers. Continue to sauté, stirring occasionally, for another 5 minutes or until vegetables are tender.

3.   Add tomato sauce, bay leaves, crushed red pepper, cilantro, salt, and pepper to pan. Stir to mix.

4.   Reduce heat to low. Make 8 wells in the pan to hold the eggs. Crack an egg gently into each well. Cover pan with lid and let simmer for 5 minutes.

5.   Remove cover and check eggs. If whites are not set, re-cover pan, and cook for an additional 2-4 minutes, checking frequently, until whites are set.

6.   Remove from heat and serve immediately.

PERFECTLY CRISPED BACON

··

Bacon can be tricky to cook in a cast iron pan but if you follow these steps your bacon should come out perfect every time.

Servings: 6

··

1 pound bacon, thick-cut

··

1.   Place skillet on burner and heat over medium-low heat. Lightly spray bottom of pan with cooking spray if pan is fairly new or skip this step if pan is well-seasoned. Separate bacon slices and place in pan, don't worry if it doesn't lie flat. As bacon cooks, use spatula to flip and stir every minute or two. Continue to cook, and as grease is released, scrape any "gummy" bits of the bottom with spatula. Cook until bacon reaches desired degree of crispiness.

2.   Remove bacon from pan and drain off excess grease on paper towels. Drain excess grease into mason jar and store for later use.

EASY SAUSAGE GRAVY AND BISCUITS

This one-dish meal is perfect for a family breakfast.

Servings: 8

1 can (16 ounce) jumbo refrigerated flaky biscuits

1 pound pork sausage

1 medium onion, chopped

2 garlic cloves, minced

4 tablespoons unsalted butter

4 tablespoons all-purpose flour

2 cups milk

1 teaspoon fresh sage, minced

1 teaspoon fresh thyme, minced

¼ cup fresh parsley, minced

Salt and freshly ground black pepper to taste

1. Bake biscuits according to package directions.

2. In a large cast iron skillet over medium high heat, cook sausage, onion, and garlic until lightly browned, about 5-6 minutes. Use a slotted spoon remove sausage from skillet and place in a bowl.

3. Reduce heat to medium low and add butter to skillet and let melt Sprinkle flour over butter and whisk together. Cook for a couple of minutes, whisking occasionally.

4. Add milk and whisk to combine. Continue to cook, stirring frequently, until mixture starts to bubble and thicken. Add sausage mixture back into skillet along with sage, thyme, parsley, salt, and pepper, and continue cooking, stirring frequently for another 3-4 minutes.

5. To serve, split biscuits in half on plate and top with sausage gravy.

BEST BUTTERMILK PANCAKES

These pancakes are light and fluffy.

Servings: 8

3 cups all-purpose flour

3 tablespoons sugar

3 teaspoons baking powder

1 ½ teaspoons baking soda

1 teaspoon salt

2 1/2 cups buttermilk

1 cup milk

1 teaspoon lemon juice

1 teaspoon vanilla

3 eggs

1/3 cup butter, melted

1.   In a mixing bowl, combine all dry ingredients. In a separate bowl, combine buttermilk, milk, lemon juice, vanilla, eggs, and melted butter.

2.   Pour wet ingredients into dry ingredients. Stir gently until just combined. Do not overmix. Let batter rest for 30 minutes in refrigerator.

3.   Heat cast iron griddle or skillet over medium-high heat. Coat with cooking spray or vegetable oil.

4.   Add 1/3 cup of batter for each pancake onto griddle. Cook until pancake is dry around the edges and bubbles form on top and bottom is golden brown. Flip and cook until other side is golden brown. Serve hot with your favorite toppings.

CHOCOLATE CHIP-BANANA-PECAN PANCAKES

....

These decadent pancakes are a real treat.

Servings: 8

....

3 cups all-purpose flour

3 tablespoons sugar

3 teaspoons baking powder

1 ½ teaspoons baking soda

1 teaspoon salt

2 1/2 cups buttermilk

1 cup milk

1 teaspoon lemon juice

1 teaspoon vanilla

3 eggs

1/3 cup butter, melted

1 banana, sliced thin

1/3 cup chopped pecans

¼ cup miniature semisweet chocolate chips

....

1.   In a mixing bowl, combine all dry ingredients. In a separate bowl, combine buttermilk, milk, lemon juice, vanilla, eggs, and melted butter.

2.   Pour wet ingredients into dry ingredients. Stir gently until just combined. Do not overmix. Let batter rest for 30 minutes in refrigerator. Before cooking, fold in banana slices, pecans and chocolate chips.

3.   Heat cast iron griddle or skillet over medium-high heat. Coat with cooking spray or vegetable oil.

4.   Add 1/3 cup of batter for each pancake onto griddle. Cook until pancake is dry around the edges and bubbles form on top and bottom is golden brown. Flip and cook until other side is golden brown. Serve hot.

BLUEBERRY-OATMEAL PANCAKES

....

A healthier take on traditional blueberry pancakes.

Servings: 8

....

1 ½ cups quick-cooking oats

½ cup whole wheat flour

½ cup all-purpose flour

3 tablespoons sugar

3 teaspoons baking powder

1 ½ teaspoons baking soda

1 teaspoon salt

2 cups milk

1 teaspoon lemon juice

3 eggs

¼ cup butter, melted

1 cup fresh blueberries

....

1.   In a mixing bowl, combine all dry ingredients. In a separate bowl, combine milk, lemon juice, eggs, and melted butter.

2.   Pour wet ingredients into dry ingredients. Stir gently until just combined. Do not overmix. Fold in blueberries. Let batter rest for 30 minutes in refrigerator.

3.   Heat cast iron griddle or skillet over medium-high heat. Coat with cooking spray or vegetable oil.

4.   Add 1/3 cup of batter for each pancake onto griddle. Cook until pancake is dry around the edges and bubbles form on top and bottom is golden brown. Flip and cook until other side is golden brown. Serve hot with your favorite toppings.

3
Main Dishes

BEST BASIC GRILLED CHEESE SANDWICH

Grilled cheese sandwiches are not just for kids. Crisp on the outside and warm and creamy on the inside, they are the ultimate comfort food. Master the basic grilled cheese sandwich and then add your own endless variations.

Servings: 1

2 slices good quality bread – try sourdough, ciabatta, or sprouted whole grain (day old bread is fine for grilled cheese)

2 slices of cheese – any type of meltable cheese will do, try cheddar, Swiss, American, Monterey Jack, even Brie will work, mix a couple together for flavor combinations

1-2 tablespoons salted butter

1.   Heat cast iron skillet or medium-low heat.

2.   Place bread on flat surface. Cover with layer of cheese, top with remaining slice of bread. Spread thin coat of butter on top slice of bread.

3.   Add 1-2 tablespoons of butter to skillet. When butter is melted place sandwich, unbuttered side down, in skillet. Grill until golden brown, flip, and grill other side until golden brown and cheese is melted, about 3-4 minutes per side.

4.   Serve hot.

GRILLED CHEESE WITH AVOCADO AND TOMATO

This is one of my favorite combinations. Use firm tomatoes to keep sandwich from getting soggy.

Servings: 2

4 slices multigrain bread

4 slices (2 ounces) sharp cheddar cheese

½ Haas avocado, peeled and sliced

4 slices of tomato

Freshly ground black pepper, to taste

Salted butter

1. Heat cast iron skillet or medium-low heat.
2. Place bread slices on flat surface. Cover with layer of cheese, tomato slices, and avocado. Season with pepper and top with slice of bread. Spread thin coat of butter on top slices of bread.
3. Add 1-2 tablespoons of butter to skillet. When butter is melted place sandwiches, unbuttered side down, in skillet. Grill until golden brown, flip, and grill other side until golden brown and cheese is melted, about 3-4 minutes per side.
4. Serve hot.

ITALIAN GRILLED CHEESE

Servings: 2

4 slices sourdough bread

2-3 ounces shredded mozzarella cheese

2 plum tomatoes, sliced

4-6 fresh basil leaves

Freshly ground black pepper, to taste

Salted butter

1. Heat cast iron skillet or medium-low heat.

2. Place bread slices on flat surface. Cover with layer of cheese, tomato slices, and fresh basil. Season with pepper and top with slice of bread. Spread thin coat of butter on top slices of bread.

3. Add 1-2 tablespoons of butter to skillet. When butter is melted place sandwiches, unbuttered side down, in skillet. Grill until golden brown, flip, and grill other side until golden brown and cheese is melted, about 3-4 minutes per side.

4. Serve hot.

PESTO, MOZZARELLA, AND ROMA TOMATO GRILLED CHEESE

Servings: 2

4 slices whole-grain bread

2 tablespoons pesto sauce

2 slices provolone cheese

2 slices mozzarella cheese

2 Roma tomatoes, sliced

Freshly ground black pepper, to taste

Salted butter

1.   Heat cast iron skillet or medium-low heat.

2.   Place bread slices on flat surface. Spread each slice with pesto sauce. Top with provolone cheese, mozzarella cheese, and tomato slices. Season with pepper and top with slice of bread. Spread thin coat of butter on top slices of bread.

3.   Add 1-2 tablespoons of butter to skillet. When butter is melted place sandwiches, unbuttered side down, in skillet. Grill until golden brown, flip, and grill other side until golden brown and cheese is melted, about 3-4 minutes per side.

4.   Serve hot.

SWISS CHEESE, MUSHROOMS, AND CARAMELIZED ONION GRILLED SANDWICH

A sophisticated take on the humble grilled cheese sandwich.

Servings: 2

4 slices whole-grain bread

4 slice Swiss cheese

½ cup sautéed mushrooms

½ cup caramelized onion (see recipe on page 111)

Freshly ground black pepper, to taste

Salted butter

1.   Heat cast iron skillet or medium-low heat.

2.   Place bread slices on flat surface. Top with slices of Swiss cheese. Top with sautéed mushrooms and caramelized onions. Season with pepper and top with slice of bread. Spread thin coat of butter on top slices of bread.

3.   Add 1-2 tablespoons of butter to skillet. When butter is melted place sandwiches, unbuttered side down, in skillet. Grill until golden brown, flip, and grill other side until golden brown and cheese is melted, about 3-4 minutes per side.

4.   Serve hot.

PEPPERONI PIZZA

....

Cooking deep-dish pizza in cast iron makes for a golden brown crust.

Servings: 1 12-inch pizza

....

1 package active dry yeast

1/2 teaspoon sugar

½ cup warm water

1 1/2 cups all-purpose flour

1 teaspoon salt

1 tablespoon olive oil

2 ounces pepperoni slices

1/2 cup pizza or marinara sauce

3/4 cup shredded mozzarella cheese

¼ cup Parmesan cheese, grated

....

1.　　Mix yeast and sugar together in small bowl with warm water. Let stand for 10 minutes.

2.　　In a food processor or high-speed blender, mix flour and salt together. Add in yeast mixture and pulse until moistened. With machine running, slowly drizzle in olive oil. Process until ball forms. Remove dough and knead on lightly floured surface for 2-3 minutes. Place dough ball in bowl that has been oiled and cover with kitchen towel. Let rise until it has doubled in size, about 45 minutes. Punch down dough and allow to rest for 20 minutes.

3.　　Preheat oven to 400 degrees F. Grease a 12-inch cast iron skillet with olive oil.

4.　　Press dough along bottom and up sides of skillet. Poke holes in dough with a fork to prevent air bubbles. Spread sauce onto crust and spread out evenly. Top with pepperoni slices and mozzarella cheese. Sprinkle Parmesan cheese over top.

5.　　Bake in oven for 25 minutes or until crust is golden brown and cheese is melted and bubbly.

DEEP-DISH SAUSAGE AND MUSHROOM PIZZA

This pizza has a thick crust and delicious fillings.

Servings: 1 12-inch pizza

1 package active dry yeast

1/2 teaspoon sugar

½ cup warm water

1 1/2 cups all-purpose flour

1 teaspoon salt

1 tablespoon olive oil

½ pound Italian sausage

1/2 cup pizza or marinara sauce

1 cup fresh mushrooms, sliced

3/4 cup shredded mozzarella cheese

¼ cup Parmesan cheese, grated

1. Mix yeast and sugar together in small bowl with warm water. Let stand for 10 minutes.

2. In a food processor or high-speed blender, mix flour and salt together. Add in yeast mixture and pulse until moistened. With machine running, slowly drizzle in olive oil. Process until ball forms. Remove dough and knead on lightly floured surface for 2-3 minutes. Place dough ball in bowl that has been oiled and cover with kitchen towel. Let rise until it has doubled in size, about 45 minutes. Punch down dough and allow to rest for 20 minutes.

3. While dough is resting, heat a cast iron skillet over medium heat. Add sausage and cook until cooked through, about 10 minutes. Remove sausage from pan, slice, and set aside.

4. Preheat oven to 400 degrees F. Grease a 12-inch cast iron skillet with olive oil.

5. Press dough along bottom and up sides of skillet. Poke holes in dough with a fork to prevent air bubbles. Spread sauce onto crust and spread out evenly. Top with sausage slices, mushrooms, and mozzarella cheese. Sprinkle Parmesan cheese over top.

6. Bake in oven for 25 minutes or until crust is golden brown and cheese is melted and bubbly.

CRISPY FRIED BUTTERMILK CHICKEN

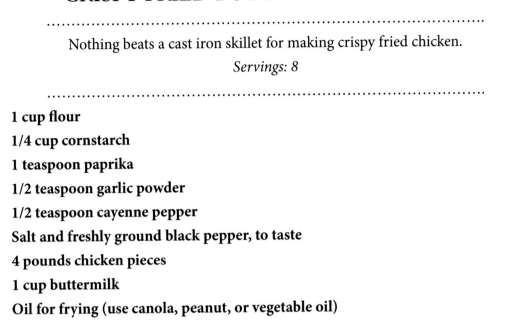

....

Nothing beats a cast iron skillet for making crispy fried chicken.

Servings: 8

....

1 cup flour

1/4 cup cornstarch

1 teaspoon paprika

1/2 teaspoon garlic powder

1/2 teaspoon cayenne pepper

Salt and freshly ground black pepper, to taste

4 pounds chicken pieces

1 cup buttermilk

Oil for frying (use canola, peanut, or vegetable oil)

....

1.   Place flour, cornstarch, paprika, garlic powder, cayenne pepper, salt, and pepper in large zipper-lock plastic bag.

2.   Pour buttermilk into bowl and dip chicken pieces in a couple at a time and then place in plastic bag with flour.

3.   Seal bag and shake to thoroughly coat chicken. Remove from bag and place on large plate or cookie sheet. Allow to sit until coating thickens and becomes paste-like.

4.   Add enough oil to 12-inch cast iron to about half-fill it. Alternatively, use a cast iron Dutch oven. Heat over high heat until it is very hot. Use thermometer to test oil hotness (350 degrees F) or if thermometer is unavailable, test hotness by adding a small piece of chicken coating to pan, if it starts to sizzle immediately the pan is ready.

5.   When oil is hot, place chicken pieces in pan (may need to be done in batches, don't crowd the pan) and fry for about 7-10 minutes per side or until crust is crispy and chicken is cooked through. Check internal temperature using meat thermometer; internal temperature should reach 165 degrees F.

6.   Drain on wire rack with paper towels spread underneath to catch excess oil.

SPAGHETTI WITH GARLIC, TOMATOES, AND THYME

Servings: 4

1 pound spaghetti

½ cup olive oil

½ medium onion, diced

4-5 garlic cloves, minced

¼ teaspoon dried red pepper flakes

12 grape tomatoes

½ teaspoon salt

1 teaspoon thyme

½ teaspoon freshly ground black pepper

1.   Bring a large pot of water to a boil, add a dash of salt, and cook spaghetti until al dente, about 10 minutes. Drain and set aside.

2.   Heat a cast iron skillet over medium-low heat. Add olive oil, onion, garlic, and red pepper. Cook, stirring, until onion softens, about 3-4 minutes. Add tomatoes, salt, thyme, and black pepper, and continue to cook, stirring occasionally, until tomatoes soften and begin to brown, about 5 minutes.

3.   Add spaghetti to skillet and toss to coat. Serve hot.

TERIYAKI CHICKEN STIR-FRY

This only takes about 15 minutes to cook so you can have dinner ready in no time.

Servings: 4

2 tablespoons vegetable oil

1 medium onion, chopped

2 cloves garlic, minced

4 boneless, skinless chicken breast, cut into small pieces

2 large carrots, peeled and sliced thin

1 red pepper, sliced thin

1 cup thin green beans

2 cups broccoli florets, cut into small pieced

1 can water chestnuts, drained

Sauce

1/3 cup soy sauce

1/4 cup honey

2 tablespoons rice wine vinegar

2 teaspoons arrowroot flour

1.   Heat oil in a large cast iron skillet or wok over medium-high heat. Add the onion and garlic and cook for 2-3 minutes until onion starts to soften. Add the chicken and cook, stirring occasionally, until chicken starts to brown, about 3-4 minutes. Add carrots, red pepper, green beans, broccoli, and water chestnuts, and continue cooking until vegetables soften, about 3-4 minutes.

2.   In a small bowl, whisk together sauce ingredients. Pour over chicken and vegetables. Continue cooking and stirring until chicken and vegetables are coated with sauce.

3.   Serve hot over rice or noodles.

CHICKEN AND MUSHROOMS

A take on the classic chicken Marsala.

Servings: 4

½ cup all-purpose flour

1 teaspoon thyme

1 teaspoon garlic powder

½ teaspoon oregano

½ teaspoon cayenne pepper

1/1 teaspoon sea salt

½ teaspoon freshly ground black pepper

2 (6-8 ounce) boneless, skinless chicken breast, cut into bite-size chunks

1 tablespoon olive oil

3 tablespoons butter

3 cups baby mushrooms, stems trimmed

1 medium yellow onion, sliced thin

8-10 grape tomatoes

1 ½ cups chicken stock

1.   In a bowl, mix together the flour, spices, salt, and pepper. Dredge chicken pieces in the flour mixture. Shake to remove excess and place on plate.

2.   In a large cast iron skillet, heat olive oil and 1 tablespoon of butter over medium-high heat. Add chicken pieces and cook until chicken is golden brown on all sides, about 5-6 minutes. Remove chicken from pan and set aside.

3.   Add another tablespoon of butter to pan and add mushrooms and onions. Cook, stirring frequently, until mushrooms have softened and onions are translucent, about 4-5 minutes. Add tomatoes and cook for an additional 1-2 minutes.

4.   Add chicken stock to pan as well as chicken pieces and remaining tablespoon of butter. Continue to cook, stirring often, until chicken has cooked through and sauce has thickened, about 4-5 minutes. Add additional salt and pepper to taste. Serve immediately.

CHICKEN, ZUCCHINI, AND PLUM TOMATO FRITTATA

Servings: 8

8 eggs, beaten

¼ cup Parmesan cheese

Sea salt and freshly ground black pepper, to taste

2 tablespoons olive oil

½ pound chicken breast or tenders, cut into bite-size chunks

2 small zucchini, sliced

½ medium yellow onion, diced

1 clove garlic, minced

3-4 plum tomatoes, chopped

1.   Preheat oven to 400 degrees F.

2.   In a bowl, whisk together eggs, Parmesan cheese, salt, and pepper. Set aside.

3.   Heat 1 tablespoon olive oil in 12-inch cast iron skillet. Add chicken pieces and cook until chicken is cooked through, about 5-6 minutes. Remove from pan and reserve.

4.   Add remaining tablespoon of olive oil, zucchini, onion, and garlic to skillet. Cook until vegetables are tender, about 4-5 minutes. Return chicken to skillet and stir to mix evenly. Pour egg mixture over chicken and vegetables, and cook for 3-4 minutes, until eggs begin to set on bottom.

5.   Place skillet in oven and bake for 10-12 minutes, or until eggs are set and top is light golden brown.

6.   Cut into 8 slices and serve.

HOW TO COOK THE PERFECT PAN-SEARED STEAK

....

Pan-searing steak is my preferred method of cooking steak, beating out even grilling. Why? Because cooking steak on a hot cast iron pan produces an even golden-brown crust that just can't be topped. In addition, pan-seared steaks retain more moisture and can be cooked alongside your favorite flavorings, like garlic and herbs.

....

Basic method:

1. Choose a thick (1 1/2 to 2 inches), marbled steak. Good ones to try include New York strip, ribeye, T-bone, or tenderloin.

2. Season steak with kosher salt.

3. Preheat cast iron pan until it is smoking hot.

4. Add generous amount of oil to pan (about a 1/4 cup) and allow to heat. I prefer olive oil.

5. Add steak to pan, and cooking, flipping occasionally and basting with pan juices often, until desired doneness is reached.

6. Add butter to pan during last few minutes along with herbs and garlic if desired for flavor.

7. Allow steak to rest before serving.

STEAK SMOTHERED IN MUSHROOMS

Sirloin steak topped with mushrooms in a balsamic sauce.

Servings: 4

1 pound sirloin steak

1 tablespoon olive oil

1 1/2 cups mushrooms, sliced

2 tablespoons butter

1/2 tablespoon all-purpose flour

Freshly ground black pepper, to taste

3 tablespoons balsamic vinegar

1.   Heat oil in large cast iron skillet over medium-high heat. Add steak and cook, turning occasionally, until desired doneness. Remove steak from pan and slice into thin strips.

2.   In same skillet, add mushrooms and butter. Sprinkle with flour and continue cooking, stirring occasionally, until mushrooms start to brown. About 5-6 minutes. Season with black pepper.

3.   Add in vinegar and cook for an additional 2 minutes, stirring frequently.

4.   Serve steak with mushroom mixture on top.

GRILLED STEAK WITH GINGER MARINADE

....

This recipe is very simple, but oh so delicious.

Servings: 4

....

1 piece of fresh ginger (about 6-inches), sliced into thin slices

1/4 cup sesame oil

8 cloves garlic, minced

2 teaspoons lemon juice

1 tablespoon honey

2 teaspoons salt

1 teaspoon freshly ground pepper

1 1/2 pounds flank steak, trimmed

2 tablespoons olive oil

....

1.   In a bowl, whisk together all ingredients except steak. Pour into large re-sealable plastic bag. Add flank steak, seal, and shake to thoroughly coat steak with marinade.

2.   Allow to marinade for 30 minutes at room temperature. Can also marinate in refrigerator for up to 24 hours.

3.   Heat olive oil in large cast iron grill pan over medium-high heat.

4.   Remove steak from marinade, allow excess marinade to drip off. Add to pan and cook to desired doneness, about 6-8 minutes per side for medium rare, 8-10 minutes for medium, and 10-12 minutes for medium well.

5.   Remove from pan and place on cutting board and let rest for 5-10 minutes. Slice, against the grain, into thin slices. Serve.

ORANGE CHICKEN AND BROCCOLI STIR FRY

Skip the Chinese takeout and serve this delicious healthy stir fry instead.

Servings: 4

1 tablespoon olive oil or coconut oil

1 pound chicken breast, boneless and skinless, cut into strips

1/3 cup orange juice

2 tablespoons low-sodium soy sauce

2 teaspoons cornstarch

2 cups broccoli, cut into small pieces

1 cup snow peas

2 cups cabbage, shredded

2 cups brown rice, cooked

1 tablespoon sesame seeds (optional)

1.   In a bowl, combine orange juice, soy sauce, and corn starch. Set aside.

2.   Heat oil in cast iron wok or skillet over high heat. Add chicken and stir fry for 4-5 minutes or until chicken is golden brown on all sides.

3.   Add broccoli, snow peas, cabbage, and sauce mixture. Continue to stir fry until vegetables are tender but still crisp, about 7-8 minutes.

4.   Serve over brown rice and sprinkle with sesame seeds.

BEEF AND VEGGIE STIR FRY WITH GINGER-ORANGE SAUCE

....

This stir fry cooks up in just 10 minutes (plus prep time) and has a delicious orange-ginger sauce.

Servings: 4

....

Marinade:

- 1/ 2 cup orange juice
- 4 tablespoons soy sauce
- 2 teaspoons sesame oil
- 2 teaspoons fresh grated ginger
- 3 garlic cloves, minced

Stir Fry:

- 1 tablespoon coconut oil (can substitute with other cooking oil)
- 1 pound flank steak, sliced into thin strips
- 1 small yellow onion, diced
- 1 red bell pepper, sliced thin
- 3 stalks celery, chopped
- 1 large carrot, cut into julienne slices
- 1 small bunch broccoli, cut into small florets
- Diced green onions, for garnish

....

1. Combine marinade ingredients in large bowl. Add steak strips and mix so steak is fully coated in marinade. Cover and refrigerate for 30 minutes.

2. Heat coconut oil in large cast iron skillet or wok over high heat. Add onion and stir fry for 1-2 minutes.

3. Remove beef from refrigerator, and drain, reserving the marinade. Add to beef to pan and stir fry for 2-3 minutes. Add onion, bell pepper, celery, carrot, broccoli, and marinade to pan. Continue cooking, stirring frequently, until veggies are tender and marinade starts to thicken.

4. Remove from heat. Top with diced green onion for garnish. Serve over bed of rice or noodles.

GLAZED PORK CHOPS WITH APRICOT-MANGO SALSA

....

These pork chops are so easy to prepare and mouth-wateringly good.

Servings: 4

....

1/3 cup Dijon mustard

3 tablespoons balsamic vinegar

1 teaspoon cumin

Salt and fresh ground black pepper, to taste

4 pork chops

2-3 tablespoons olive oil

For the Apricot-Mango Salsa

4 fresh apricots, pit removed, diced

1 ripe mango, peeled, diced

1/4 red onion, diced small

1/4 cup fresh basil, minced

1/4 cup extra virgin olive oil

1 teaspoon cardamom

....

1. In a bowl, mix mustard, vinegar, and cumin.

2. Sprinkle both sides of pork chops with salt and pepper. Brush mustard mixture onto pork chops, covering both sides.

3. Heat olive oil in cast iron grill pan or skillet over medium high heat. Add pork chops over cook for about 5 minutes per side, or until cooked through. Baste with mustard sauce when they're flipped.

4. While pork chops are cooking, mix together ingredients for salsa in a bowl.

5. When pork chops are finished, top with salsa.

EASY, TASTY LAMB CHOPS

These lamb chops can be made start to finish in less than half hour.

Servings: 4

2 garlic cloves, crushed

1 tablespoon rosemary, crushed

1 teaspoon thyme

2 tablespoons Dijon mustard

2 tablespoons lemon juice plus additional slices for garnish

3 tablespoons olive oil

1 tablespoon ghee

4 lamb chops (about 1-inch thick)

Salt and freshly ground black pepper, to taste

1.   In a bowl, combine garlic, rosemary, thyme, mustard, lemon juice, and 1 tablespoon of the olive oil. Stir until well blended. Spread mixture over lamb chops, coating both sides thoroughly. Let marinate for 20 minutes at room temperature.

2.   Heat remaining olive oil and ghee in a large cast iron skillet or grill pan over high heat. When pan is very hot, add lamb chops and sear for 2-3 minutes. Flip chops over and cook for an additional 3-4 minutes or until desired level of doneness. Serve garnished with lemon slices.

PAN-SEARED SALMON ON BABY ARUGULA

Make sure your pan is well-seasoned before attempting to sear fish.

Servings: 2

2 (6 oz.) salmon fillets

1 1/2 tablespoons olive oil

1 1/2 tablespoons fresh lemon juice

Freshly ground black pepper, to taste

For the salad:

3 cups baby arugula leaves

2/3 cup grape or cherry tomatoes, halved

1/4 cup red onion, thinly slivered

1 tablespoon extra-virgin olive oil

1 tablespoon red-wine vinegar

1.   In a bowl, marinate salmon with mixture of olive oil, lemon juice, and pepper. Let stand for at least 15 minutes.

2.   In a cast iron skillet heated over medium-high heat, cook salmon skin side down, for about 3 minutes. Loosen any sticking skin. Lower heat, cover, and continue cooking for about 3 minutes more or until just firm and skin is crispy.

3.   Prepare salad by combining the arugula, onion, and tomatoes in a bowl. Add oil and vinegar then season with pepper. Serve at once with the fish.

SAUSAGE, APPLE, AND CABBAGE SKILLET

....

Servings: 4

....

1 tablespoon olive oil

1 pound kielbasa sausage, cut into 1-inch slices

1 medium yellow onion, diced

3 Golden Delicious apples, peeled, cored, and chopped

6 cups cabbage, coarsely shredded

1 cup low-sodium chicken broth

1 teaspoon Dijon mustard

Sea salt and freshly ground black pepper, to taste

....

1.	Heat oil in cast iron skillet over medium heat. Add sausage and cook until browned. Remove from pan and set aside.

2.	Add onion, apple, and cabbage and sauté for 8-10 minutes. Add sausage, chicken broth, Dijon mustard, salt, and pepper. Stir, reduce heat, and simmer for 10 minutes, or until cabbage is tender.

3.	Serve hot.

OVEN-BARBECUED PORK CHOPS

When it's too cold outside for the grill, cook these up for an indoor barbecue.

Servings: 4

4 bone-in 3/4-inch thick pork chops (about 1 1/2 pounds)

1/4 teaspoon salt

1/4 teaspoon freshly ground black pepper

1 tablespoon plus 1 teaspoon olive oil

1 medium onion, diced

3 cloves garlic, minced

1/3 cup orange juice

1/2 cup low-sodium barbecue sauce

1.   Preheat oven to 400 degrees F.

2.   Heat 1 tablespoon olive oil in cast iron grill pan or skillet over high heat. Add pork chops, season with salt and pepper, and cook until browned, 1 to 2 minutes per side. Transfer to plate.

3.   Add remaining 1 teaspoon olive oil to pan. Add onion and garlic and cook, stirring, until softened, 3-4 minutes. Add orange juice and continue cooking until most of liquid is evaporated, 2-3 minutes. Add in barbecue sauce, stir.

4.   Return pork chops to pan, turning to coat with sauce.

5.   Transfer pan to oven and bake until pork chops are cooked (internal temperature of 145 F), about 7-8 minutes.

6.   Serve pork chops topped with sauce.

SHEPHERD'S PIE

This shepherd's pie uses beef instead of the traditional lamb. Ground turkey would also be a good substitute.

Servings: 8

1 ½ pounds potatoes, peeled and cubed

1 pound ground beef

3 cloves garlic, chopped

½ yellow onion, diced

½ cup fresh mushrooms, sliced

2 tablespoons flour

1 cup low-sodium beef broth

3 tablespoons ketchup

1 tablespoon Worcestershire sauce

½ teaspoon thyme

½ teaspoon paprika

1 cup green beans, fresh or frozen

Sea salt and freshly ground black pepper, to taste

½ cup shredded Cheddar cheese

¾ cup light sour cream

1.	Place potatoes in large pot and cover with water. Bring to boil, reduce heat to medium, and simmer, covered for 15-20 minutes, or until potatoes are tender. Drain.

2.	Heat cast iron skillet over medium heat. Add ground beef, onion, and mushrooms, and cook, stirring occasionally, until beef is browned. Stir in flour.

3.	Add broth, ketchup, Worcestershire sauce, thyme, paprika, and beans. Stir, and season with salt and pepper. Cook for 5 minutes, until sauce begins to thicken.

4.	Mash potatoes coarsely and add ¼ cup cheese and sour cream. Mix until creamy. Spread potato mixture on top of beef and vegetable mixture. Sprinkle with remaining cheese.

5.	Bake in preheated 375 degree F. oven for 20-25 minutes or until cheese is melted and light golden brown.

STEAK TACOS

Authentic-style Mexican tacos.

Servings: 6

1 1/4 pounds sirloin steak, cut into strips

1/4 teaspoon salt

Freshly ground black pepper, to taste

2 tablespoons plus 2 teaspoons olive oil

12 (6-inch) tortillas

1/2 red onion, diced

3 fresh jalapeno peppers, seeded and chopped

1/2 bunch fresh cilantro, chopped

3 limes, cut into wedges

1.   In a large cast iron skillet, heat 2 tablespoons olive oil over medium-high heat. Add steak and sauté until browned on all sides and cooked through to desired doneness, about 5-6 minutes. Season with salt and pepper. Remove from pan to plate and cover to keep warm.

2.   In same skillet, add 2 more teaspoons olive oil and allow to get hot. Add tortillas, one at a time, and cook turning once, until tortilla is lightly browned but still flexible.

3.   To assemble tacos, place tortilla on a plate and top with steak, onion, jalapeno peppers, and cilantro. Squeeze lime juice over top.

PRIME RIB ROAST IN A SKILLET

Servings: 8

1 (4-5 pound) beef prime rib roast

Sea salt and freshly ground black pepper

1 large onion, quartered

1/4 cup unsalted butter

1/4 cup all-purpose flour

1/4 cup red wine

4 cups beef stock

1 ½ teaspoons thyme

1.   Preheat oven to 300 degrees F.

2.   Sprinkle roast with salt and black pepper.

3.   Heat a large cast-iron skillet over medium-high heat. Sear roast on all sides in the skillet, about 2 to 3 minutes per side.

4.   Scatter onion around roast and cook prime rib, ribs side up, in oven for 2-3 hours, until internal temperature reads 130 degrees F.

5.   Remove roast to large platter, wrap in aluminum foil, and let rest for 15 to 20 minutes.

6.   Leave onion in skillet and skim off excess grease from top of pan drippings. Place over medium heat and melt butter in the drippings. Sprinkle in flour and whisk until mixture thickens, about 1 to 2 minutes. Stir in red wine and mix until smooth. Add beef stock and thyme and continue to stir until gravy is smooth.

7.   Reduce heat to low and simmer until gravy has thickened, about 5 to 6 minutes. Serve over prime rib.

LEMON CHICKEN AND POTATOES

Servings: 4

···

2 tablespoons olive oil, divided

lemon, sliced thin

4 cloves garlic, minced

Sea salt and black pepper, to taste

4 boneless skinless chicken breast, cut into strips

½ teaspoon rosemary

1 pound fingerling potatoes, halved

8 roma tomatoes

···

1.   Preheat oven to 450 degrees F.

2.   Coat cast iron skillet with 1 tablespoon of olive oil. Add lemon slices in single layer.

3.   In a bowl, combine garlic, salt, and pepper. Add chicken and toss to coat. Arrange chicken in skillet over lemon slices.

4.   Place potatoes in bowl and drizzle with remaining tablespoon of olive oil. Sprinkle with rosemary, salt, and pepper. Place potatoes in layer on top of chicken.

5.   Bake in preheated oven for 25-30 minutes, uncovered, until chicken is cooked through and potatoes are tender.

BARBECUED CHICKEN DRUMSTICKS

Turn up the spice as much, or as little, as you like.

Servings: 4

8 chicken drumsticks

1/3 cup ketchup

1/3 cup white vinegar

1/3 cup maple sugar

1 tablespoon butter, melted

1 teaspoon salt

2 teaspoons Worcestershire sauce

2 teaspoons dry mustard

3 teaspoons chili powder (or to taste)

Dash of hot sauce (optional)

1. Preheat oven to 400 degrees F.
2. Place drumsticks in cast iron baking dish or skillet.
3. In a bowl, whisk together ketchup, vinegar, maple syrup, butter, salt, Worcestershire sauce, mustard, chili powder, and hot sauce. Pour mixture over drumsticks, turning to coat. Cover with foil and bank in oven until internal temperature reaches 165 degrees F, about 1 hour. Remove foil for last 15 minutes so skin will brown.

EASY CHEESY TUNA NOODLE SKILLET

Servings: 6

1 box penne pasta

4 cups water

1 can cream of celery soup

2 (6 ounce) cans tuna, drained

4 cups frozen vegetables – peas, carrots, beans

½ teaspoon thyme

¼ teaspoon dill

1 cup shredded cheese (cheddar, Monterey Jack, or blend)

1.   Bring water to boil in Dutch oven or deep skillet. Add pasta, reduce heat to medium-low, and simmer, covered for 10 minutes. Do not drain.

2.   Add soup, tuna, vegetables, thyme, and dill. Stir well. Bring to boil and then reduce heat to low. Cover and simmer for 3-4 minutes. Stir in cheese, mix, and cook for another minute or two until cheese is melted.

Optional: Place under broiler for 1-2 minutes after cheese is added for golden crust.

CHICKEN AND MUSHROOM RISOTTO

Servings: 4

2 pounds chicken tenders, cut into bite-size pieces

2 tablespoons olive oil

¾ cup Arborio rice

½ medium yellow onion, diced

1 cup fresh mushrooms, sliced thin

½ green bell pepper, chopped

½ zucchini, chopped

Sea salt and freshly ground black pepper, to taste

2 cups chicken stock (may need a little more or less)

¼ cup Parmesan cheese, grated

1.   Heat olive oil in cast iron skillet over medium-high heat. Add chicken and cook until chicken is browned, about 5 minutes. Remove and set aside.

2.   Add rice, onion, mushrooms, bell pepper, and zucchini to skillet. Season with salt and pepper. Cook, stirring occasionally, for 3-4 minutes until rice is turning golden and vegetable begin to soften.

3.   Reduce heat to low and add chicken stock, ½ cup at a time to skillet. Stir and let simmer while rice absorbs liquid. Continue to add more stock until rice is tender.

4.   Add chicken to skillet along with Parmesan cheese. Stir to combine. Serve hot.

SKILLET BEEF CUBES

Serve with garlic mashed potatoes, yum!

Servings: 4

1 pound beef tenderloin, cut into 1-inch cubes

Salt and freshly ground black pepper, to taste

2 tablespoons olive oil

½ medium onion, diced

2 garlic cloves, minced

1 cup beef broth

1.   Sprinkle beef cubes with salt and pepper.

2.   Heat olive oil in cast iron skillet over medium-high heat. Add onion and garlic to skillet and sauté for 3-4 minutes, until onion begins to soften. Add beef cubes to skillet and brown on all sides.

3.   Add beef broth to pan, reduce heat to medium-low, and simmer until beef reaches desired doneness, about 10 minutes.

ROASTED CHICKEN WITH VEGETABLES AND HERBS

Cast iron is perfect for roasting this classic dish.

Servings: 4-6

1 (3 to 4 pound) whole chicken

2-3 tablespoons olive oil or softened butter

Salt and freshly ground black pepper

1 lemon, cut in half

2-3 sprigs fresh rosemary

2-3 sprigs fresh thyme

4-6 cloves garlic

1 red onion, chopped

1 small bunch baby carrots, washed

8 baby potatoes, cut in half

1.   Preheat oven to 400 degrees F.

2.   Remove giblets from inside of chicken and rinse chicken under cold running water. Pat dry with paper towels.

3.   Rub chicken all over with generous amount of olive oil or softened butter. Sprinkle with salt and pepper. Place lemon and herbs inside of chicken.

4.   Lightly oil bottom of large cast iron skillet. Spread garlic onion, carrots and potatoes in bottom of skillet. Place chicken, breast side up, into pan on top of vegetables.

5.   Put in oven and roast for between 60 to 90 minutes, depending on the size of chicken. Chicken is done when internal temperature reads 165 degrees F.

6.   Remove from oven and allow to rest for about 10 minutes before carving.

CRISPY COCONUT CHICKEN FINGERS WITH HONEY MUSTARD SAUCE

These are so good you might want to make a double batch.

Servings: 3-4

1 pound chicken tenderloins

1 egg

1/2 cup almond flour

1 cup shredded coconut, unsweetened

1/2 teaspoon salt

2 tablespoons coconut oil

Mustard Sauce, for dipping

1.   In a bowl, whisk the egg. In a separate bowl, combine almond flour, coconut, and salt.

2.   Dip chicken strips into egg and then coat with almond-coconut mixture.

3.   Heat a large skillet over medium-high heat. Add coconut oil to pan and let heat.

4.   Add chicken strips to pan and cook until light browned on one side, about 3-4 minutes. Flip chicken over and cook another 4 minutes or until chicken is cooked all the way through.

5.   Serve with Honey Mustard Sauce for dipping.

Honey Mustard Sauce

Servings: About 1 cup of sauce

Ingredients

1/2 cup extra-virgin olive oil

¼ cup apple cider vinegar

2 tablespoons brown mustard

2 tablespoons Dijon mustard

3 tablespoons honey (use more or less depending on desired sweetness)

1 teaspoon sea salt

1 teaspoon freshly ground black pepper

Directions

Whisk all ingredients together in a bowl. Store in glass container in refrigerator.

CHICKEN AND PEPPER FAJITAS

These sizzling fajitas have a zesty flavor that are sure to make them a hit.

Servings: 6

Marinade

> 1/4 cup olive oil
>
> 2 tablespoons Worcestershire sauce
>
> Juice of 2 limes
>
> 1 teaspoon cumin
>
> 1/2 teaspoon salt
>
> 1/2 teaspoon freshly ground black pepper
>
> 3 garlic cloves, minced
>
> 2 cups low-sodium chicken broth
>
> Dash of hot sauce (optional)

Fajitas

> 2 tablespoons olive oil
>
> 2 pounds chicken tenders
>
> 2 green bell peppers, sliced into thin strips
>
> 2 red bell peppers, sliced into thin strips
>
> 1 large onion (Vidalia preferred), sliced
>
> 12 flour tortillas

For serving: Salsa, sour cream, fresh cilantro, lime wedges

1.   In a bowl, whisk together all ingredients for marinade. Divide marinade between two zip lock bags. Add chicken tenders to one bag and peppers and onions to second bag. Seal bags and shake to mix. Refrigerate for a minimum of 4 hours.

2.   When ready to cook, remove chicken and vegetables from zip-lock bags, discard marinade.

3.   Heat 2 tablespoons olive oil in large cast iron skillet over medium-high heat. Add peppers and onions and sauté for 4-5 minutes. Add chicken tenders and continue to cook, stirring occasionally, until chicken is cooked through and vegetables are tender, about 7-8 minutes.

4.   Heat oven to 300 degrees F. Wrap tortillas in foil and place in oven for 2-3 minutes, until warm.

5.   To serve: Slice chicken in to thin slices. For each fajita, place one tortilla on plate, add chicken, onions, and peppers. Top with salsa, sour cream, fresh cilantro, and squeeze of lime.

SKILLET MAC AND CHEESE

Rich and creamy, this is the best mac and cheese you've ever tasted.

Servings: 4-6

3/4 pound penne

3 tablespoons butter

2 cloves garlic, minced

1 1/2 cups half-and-half

2 tablespoons all-purpose flour

8 ounces shredded sharp cheddar cheese

1/2 cup grated Parmesan cheese, plus 2 tablespoons

2 tablespoons sour cream

1 teaspoon Dijon mustard

Salt and freshly ground black pepper, to taste

1/4 cup Panko bread crumbs

1. Preheat oven to 400 degrees F.

2. In a large pot, cook penne according to package directions until al dente. Drain and return to pot.

3. In a saucepan, melt butter over medium heat. Add garlic and sauté for 1-2 minutes. Pour in half-and-half and bring to simmer. Sprinkle in flour and whisk until smooth and mixture begins to thicken, about 3 minutes. Reduce heat to low and add cheddar cheese, 1/2 cup Parmesan cheese, sour cream, mustard, salt, and pepper. Cook, stirring often, until cheese has melted.

4. Pour cheese mixture over penne. Stir to coat evenly. Pour pasta and cheese mixture into cast iron skillet. Sprinkle with remaining Parmesan cheese and bread crumbs.

5. Bake for 20-25 minutes, until golden brown. Serve hot.

CHICKEN FRIED STEAK WITH GRAVY

....

Southern-style goodness.

Servings: 4

....

For the steaks

    4 beef cube steaks

    1 cup all-purpose flour

    1/4 cup cornmeal

    1 teaspoon freshly ground black pepper

    1/2 teaspoon salt

    1/2 cup milk

    2 eggs

    1 tablespoon hot sauce

    4 tablespoons vegetable oil

For the milk gravy

    Pan drippings

    1 tablespoon all-purpose flour

    2 cups milk or cream

    Salt and freshly ground black pepper

....

1.   In a shallow dish, combine flour, cornmeal, pepper, and salt. In another dish combine milk, eggs, and hot sauce. Coat each steak in the milk mixture and then in the flour mixture.

2.   Heat vegetable oil in a large cast iron skillet over medium heat. Add steaks and cook for 5-6 minutes per side, flipping once, or until desired doneness is reached. Remove steaks from skillet, set on plate and cover to keep warm.

3.   Sprinkle tablespoon of flour in to same skillet used to fry steaks. Whisk with pan drippings until smooth. Slowly pour in milk or cream and continue to stir until gravy starts to thicken. Reduce heat to low, season with salt and pepper, and simmer, stirring occasionally, for 5-6 minutes.

4.   Pour hot gravy over steaks and serve with mashed potatoes and biscuits.

CHILI CON CARNE WITH CHEESE

Beans are added to this traditional Texas chili recipe.

Servings: 8 to 10

2 1/2 pounds ground beef

1 large yellow onion, chopped

4 cloves garlic, minced

2 tablespoons chili powder

1 tablespoon cumin

1 tablespoon dried oregano

1 teaspoon cayenne pepper

1/2 teaspoon sea salt

1 teaspoon freshly ground black pepper

2 cups tomato sauce

3 tablespoons tomato paste

1 can (14.5 ounces) diced tomatoes

3 cups beef broth

1 tablespoon brown sugar

2 cans kidney beans, rinsed and drained

Grated cheddar cheese, for topping

1.   Heat a Dutch oven over medium-high heat. Add ground beef, onion, and garlic and cook, stirring, until beef is browned. Drain excess fat.

2.   Add chili powder, oregano, cayenne pepper, salt, pepper, tomato sauce, tomato paste, diced tomatoes, beef broth, sugar, and beans. Stir, reduce heat to low, cover, and simmer for 2 to 3 hours, stirring occasionally.

3.   Serve in bowls topped with shredded cheddar cheese.

BEEF STEW

This rich-tasting stew has a wonderful aroma.

Servings: 8

2 tablespoons olive oil

3 pounds beef cubes (sirloin, rump roast, chuck roast would all work for this)

1 medium onion, diced

4 cloves garlic, minced

1 cup dry red wine

1 teaspoon Worcestershire sauce

Juice of 1/2 lemon

1 tablespoon tomato paste

2 bay leaves

1/2 teaspoon allspice

1/2 teaspoon paprika

1 teaspoon sugar

2 cups beef broth

1 cup baby carrots

1 cup pearl onions, peeled

8 small red potatoes, cubed

1 cup button mushrooms, stems removed, washed, cubed

1.   Heat olive oil in cast iron Dutch oven over medium high heat. Add beef cubes and cook until browned on all sides. Remove and set aside.

2.   Add garlic and onion and sauté until softened, about 3-4 minutes. Add wine, Worcestershire sauce, lemon juice, tomato paste, bay leaves, allspice, paprika, sugar, and beef broth. Stir to mix. Return beef cubes to pot. Reduce heat to low, cover, and simmer for 2 hours.

3.   Add baby carrots, onions, potatoes, and mushrooms to pot. Stir, and continue cooking for another hour, until vegetables and meat are tender.

4.   Serve hot with crusty bread or over egg noodles.

CHEESEBURGER MAC AND CHEESE

So much better than boxed hamburger helpers!

Servings: 4

....

1 1/2 pounds ground beef

1 medium onion, chopped

1 green or red pepper, chopped

3 cloves garlic, minced

1 teaspoon oregano

3/4 cup dry elbow macaroni

1 1/2 cups beef stock or water

2 teaspoons Worcestershire sauce

2 tablespoons ketchup

Dash of hot sauce (optional)

2 cups shredded sharp cheddar cheese

Salt and freshly ground black pepper, to taste

....

1.   Preheat oven to 375 degrees F.

2.   Heat large cast iron skillet over medium-high heat. Add ground beef and brown for 2-3 minutes. Add onion, pepper, and garlic and continue to cook, stirring frequently until vegetables soften, about 4-5 minutes. Drain excess fat. Season with oregano and stir.

3.   Add in macaroni, beef stock or water, Worcestershire sauce, ketchup, and hot sauce. Stir, bring to low boil, reduce heat to low and simmer until macaroni is cooked (add additional stock or water if needed).

4.   Stir in shredded cheese and season with salt and pepper.

5.   Place in oven and bake for 10-15 minutes until cheese is bubbly and golden. Serve hot.

DUTCH OVEN BABY BACK RIBS

Serve with cornbread to mop up the sauce.

Servings: 6

1 tablespoon olive oil

1 large onion, chopped

3 cloves garlic, minced

2 1/2 cups ketchup

1 cup beef broth

2 tablespoons Worcestershire sauce

2 teaspoons dry mustard

1/4 cup brown sugar

1 tablespoon hot sauce (or to taste)

5 pounds baby back ribs

1.   Preheat oven to 300 degrees F.

2.   Heat oil in Dutch oven over medium-high heat. Add onion and garlic and sauté for 3-4 minutes.

3.   Add ketchup, broth, Worcestershire sauce, dry mustard, sugar, and hot sauce. Cook, stirring often, for 5 minutes.

4.   Add ribs, stir, cover and cook in oven for 2 to 2 1/2 hours, until ribs are tender.

BAKED POLENTA WITH SAUSAGE

Simple and delicious, if you've never baked polenta before try it out and see what you've been missing.

Servings: 6

1 tablespoon olive oil

1/2 pound Italian sausage, casing removed

1 small yellow onion, chopped

2 cloves garlic, minced

1 tablespoon oregano

1 tablespoon thyme

4 1/2 cups water

1 1/2 cups coarse cornmeal

2 tablespoons butter, unsalted

1/3 cup Parmesan cheese

Sea salt and freshly ground black pepper, to taste

1.   Preheat oven to 350 degrees F.

2.   Heat olive oil in cast iron skillet over medium-high heat. Add sausage and brown. Remove sausage and set aside.

3.   Add onion and garlic to skillet and sauté for 3 to 4 minutes, until vegetables soften. Season with oregano and thyme. Add this mixture to sausage, stir, and set aside.

4.   In a saucepan, bring water to boil. Add cornmeal, reduce heat to medium, and cook while stirring continuously for 5 minutes. Add butter, Parmesan cheese, salt, and pepper, stir, and remove from heat.

5.   Spread half of cornmeal into bottom of skillet, top with sausage and onion mixture. Spread remaining cornmeal on top.

6.   Bake in oven for 20-25 minutes. Let stand 5 minutes before cutting.

BLACKENED TILAPIA

1 teaspoon cayenne pepper

1 teaspoon paprika

1 teaspoon dry mustard

1 teaspoon cumin

1 teaspoon freshly ground black pepper

1 teaspoon sea salt

1 teaspoon garlic powder

1 teaspoon onion powder

 teaspoon oregano

4 tilapia fillets

3 tablespoons olive oil

1.   In a shallow bowl mix all seasoning together. Dip each tilapia fillet in sea-sonings, making sure to coat both sides completely.

2.   Heat oil in large cast iron skillet over medium-high heat. Fry fillets in oil for 3-4 minutes per side. Serve hot.

CAST IRON BURGERS

Simple and delicious, cast iron produces the best burgers around.

Servings: 4

1 pound ground beef (sirloin preferred)

1/2 teaspoon sea salt

1/2 teaspoon freshly ground black pepper

1 tablespoon olive oil

4 sesame seed hamburger buns

Toppings: Your choice of caramelized onions, sautéed mushrooms, bacon, sliced red onions, fresh tomatoes, cheddar cheese, or whatever you prefer.

1. Divide beef into 4 equal portion and form into patties about 1/2 inch thick. Sprinkle with salt and pepper.

2. Heat oil in a large cast iron skillet over medium heat. When pan is hot, add burgers and cook for 4 minutes. Flip once and cook for another 3-4 minutes or to desired degree of doneness. Add cheese if using for last minute of cooking.

3. Serve on toasted bun and top with your choice of toppings.

4
Sides

CORNBREAD

This is a simple, classic cast iron cornbread.

Servings: 8

1 ¼ cups milk

1 cup cornmeal

1 cup all-purpose flour

4 teaspoons baking powder

¾ teaspoon sea salt

1/3 cup sugar

2 eggs, beaten

¼ cup butter, melted

1 tablespoon vegetable oil

1. Preheat oven to 425 degrees F.
2. In a small bowl, mix together milk and cornmeal. Set aside.
3. In a large bowl, mix flour, baking powder, salt, and sugar. Add eggs, butter, and milk and cornmeal mixture and mix until batter is smooth.
4. Heat vegetable oil in 10-inch cast iron skillet over medium-high heat.
5. Remove skillet from burner and pour batter into skillet.
6. Bake in oven 18-22 minutes or until toothpick inserted in center comes out clean.

TANGY ROASTED BROCCOLI WITH GARLIC

....

Servings: 6

....

2 heads broccoli, cut into florets

1 clove garlic, minced

2 teaspoon extra-virgin olive oil

1 teaspoon sea salt

1/2 teaspoon ground black pepper

1/2 teaspoon lemon juice

....

1.   Preheat oven to 400 0F.

2.   In a bowl, combine oil, garlic salt, and black pepper. Add broccoli. Toss to coat.

3.   Evenly scatter broccoli in cast iron skillet and roast for about 18 minutes or until fork tender.

4.   Plate and drizzle with lemon juice. Serve at once.

CARAMELIZED ONIONS

2 tablespoons olive oil
2 Vivaldi onions, sliced thinly
Pinch of kosher salt
Pinch of black pepper
2 tablespoons sugar

1.   Heat oil in cast iron skillet over medium-high heat. Add onions, salt, and pepper and cook, stirring occasionally, until onions are soft and light golden in color, about 12-15 minutes. Add sugar and cook for another 3-4 minutes or until sugar starts to caramelize.

SAUTÉED BUTTON MUSHROOMS

These mushrooms make a delicious accompaniment to steak.

Servings: 4

2 tablespoons butter

1 tablespoon olive oil

1 pound button mushrooms, washed, stems trimmed

2 cloves garlic, minced

¼ teaspoon oregano

½ tablespoon balsamic vinegar

Heat butter and oil in skillet over medium heat. Add mushrooms, garlic, oregano, and vinegar.

Cook, stirring occasionally, until mushrooms are tender, about 20 minutes.

CORN TORTILLAS

Masa harina is a finely ground corn flour that is used to make tortillas. It can be found in most supermarkets.

Servings: 12 tortillas

1 3/4 cups masa harina

1 1/8 cups water

1.   In a medium bowl, mix together masa harina and hot water until thoroughly combined.

2.   Spread dough onto a clean surface and knead until pliable and smooth. Add more masa harina if need.

3.   Cover dough tightly with plastic wrap and allow to stand for 30 minutes.

4.   Preheat a cast iron skillet over medium-high heat.

5.   Divide dough into 12 equal-size balls. Roll out into thin flat tortillas.

6.   Immediately place tortilla in preheated pan and allow to cook for about 30 seconds, or until browned and slightly puffy. Flip and cook for another 30 seconds until second side is browned. Remove to plate and cover with towel to keep warm.

7.   Repeat until all tortillas are cooked.

FRIED BRUSSELS SPROUTS

1 pound Brussels sprouts, whole

5 tablespoon coconut oil

4 garlic cloves, minced

Dash of lemon juice, for garnish

Sea salt, to taste

Black pepper, to taste

1. In a cast iron skillet, heat oil over medium heat. Add whole Brussel sprouts, stir and cook for about 5 minutes or until browned but not charred.

2. Mix in garlic and cook for another minute or until garlic turns light brown. Sprinkle salt and pepper to taste. Drizzle lemon juice. Serve warm.

Optional: Add some shredded coconut along with garlic for a different flavor.

5
Desserts

PINEAPPLE UPSIDE DOWN CAKE

¼ cup butter

2/3 cup brown sugar, packed

1 (20 ounce) can sliced pineapple, drained

1 ¼ cups all-purpose flour

1 ½ teaspoon baking powder

½ teaspoon salt

1 cup sugar

1/3 cup shortening

1/2 cup milk

¼ cup orange juice

1 teaspoon vanilla

1 egg

1. Preheat oven to 350 degrees F.

2. Melt butter in cast-iron skillet over medium heat. Add brown sugar to skillet and stir into melted butter. Remove from heat.

3. Place pineapple slices into bottom of skillet.

4. In a bowl, mix together flour, baking powder, and salt. Add in sugar, shortening, milk, juice, vanilla, and egg. Beat until smooth.

5. Pour batter over pineapples. Bake for 35-40 minutes or until toothpick inserted in center comes out clean.

SKILLET APPLE PIE

Just like Grandmas!

Servings: 8

½ cup plus 1 tablespoon butter

1 cup brown sugar

5-6 large apples (Granny Smith, Golden delicious, Gala), peeled, cored, and sliced

1 cup sugar, divided

2 teaspoons ground cinnamon

3 9-inch pie crusts

1.   Preheat oven to 350 degrees F.

2.   Melt butter in cast iron skillet over medium heat. Add brown sugar and mix with melted butter. Remove from heat.

3.   In a bowl, mix together apples, ¾ cup white sugar, and cinnamon.

4.   Spread one pie crust in bottom of skillet over brown sugar mixture. Add ½ of apple mixture. Spread second pie crust on top. Spread second half of apple mixture on top. Layer with final pie crust.

5.   Sprinkle top with remaining ¼ cup of sugar and dot with butter. Cut slits in top.

6.   Bake in oven for 45 minutes or until crust is golden brown and apples are tender.

CHOCOLATE CHIP COOKIE CAKE

What could be better than a giant chocolate chip cookie?

Servings: 8

1 3/4 cups all-purpose flour

1 teaspoon baking soda

1/2 teaspoon salt

1 1/2 sticks butter, softened

1/2 cup sugar

3/4 cup brown sugar, packed

1 large egg

1 1/2 teaspoon vanilla extract

9 ounces semisweet chocolate chips

1. Preheat oven to 375 degrees.

2. In a bowl, mix together flour, baking soda, and salt. In a separate bowl, cream together butter, sugar, and brown sugar. Add egg and vanilla extract and mix until smooth. Slowly add in flour mixture until combined. Gently fold in chocolate chips.

3. Lightly grease 10-inch cast iron skillet with butter. Spread dough evenly in bottom of skillet.

4. Bake in oven for 40-45 minutes or until golden brown. Cool on wire rack before cutting.

PEAR TART TATIN

Cooking this French classic dessert in a cast iron skillet makes for a simple yet elegant dessert.

Servings: 8

6 pears, peeled, cored, and sliced

1/2 cup sugar

4 tablespoons butter

1 1/2 teaspoons cinnamon

1 sheet frozen puff pastry

1.   Preheat oven to 375 degrees F.

2.   Heat cast iron skillet over medium heat. Add sugar, butter, and cinnamon, and cook until butter is melted and sugar caramelizes. Add pears and continue to cook, stirring occasionally for10-12 minutes. Remove from heat.

3.   Spread pastry sheet out on lightly floured surface. Cut out circle slightly larger than skillet (use plate to guide you).

4.   Arrange pears around the edges of skillet forming a circle. Place pastry over pears, tucking edges underneath. Pierce pastry with fork several times.

5.   Bake in oven for 25-30 minutes until tart is golden brown. Let cool for 10-15 minutes in skillet before serving.

MEYER LEMON SKILLET CAKE

3/4 cup white sugar

Zest of 2 Meyer lemons, grated

Juice of 1 Meyer lemon

1/2 teaspoon vanilla

1 large egg

1/2 teaspoon baking powder

1/2 teaspoon salt

3/4 cup all-purpose flour

6 tablespoons unsalted butter, melted

1.   Preheat oven to 350 degrees F. Lightly grease bottom of 10-inch skillet.

2.   In a bowl, mix together sugar and lemon zest. Add lemon juice, vanilla, and egg and beat until smooth.

3.   In another bowl, mix together baking powder, salt, and flour. Slowly add this into wet batter. Pour in melted butter and mix until smooth.

4.   Pour batter into prepared skillet and bake in oven for 25-30 minutes or until cake is light golden. Cool before slicing.

SKILLET MONKEY BREAD

Kids love this simple treat!

Servings: 8

3/4 cup white sugar

2 teaspoons cinnamon

2 (12 ounce) packages of refrigerated biscuit dough

4 tablespoons butter, melted

3/4 cup brown sugar, packed

1/2 cup raisins

1.   Preheat oven to 350 degrees F. Lightly grease 10-inch skillet.

2.   In a shallow bowl, mix together white sugar and cinnamon. Cut biscuits into quarters and drop, in batches, into sugar mix. Mix to coat and then place in skillet. Sprinkle raisins on top of biscuits.

3.   Add brown sugar to melted butter and mix to combine. Pour over biscuits.

4.   Bake for 30-35 minutes or until golden brown. Let cool for 5 minutes and then slide onto plate. Pull apart to serve.

FUDGY SKILLET BROWNIES

Just try to eat just one of these addicting brownies!

Servings: 8

1 cup all-purpose flour

1/4 cup cocoa powder

1/2 teaspoon salt

1 1/2 cups sugar

3 large eggs

1 teaspoon vanilla

1/2 cup butter, melted

1/4 cup heavy cream

1 cup semisweet chocolate chips

1.   Preheat oven to 350 degrees F. Lightly grease 10-inch cast iron skillet.

2.   In a mixing bowl combine flour, cocoa powder, and salt.

3.   In another bowl, combine sugar, eggs, vanilla, melted butter, and cream. Slowly add in flour mixture until fully combines. Fold in chocolate chips.

4.   Pour brownie batter into skillet and bake for 30-35 minutes or until toothpick inserted in center comes out clean.

5.   Serve topped with ice cream.

From the Author

Thank you for reading the *Cast Iron Cookbook: The Ultimate Guide to Cast Iron Cooking.* I sincerely hope that you found this book informative and helpful and that it helps you to create delicious foods for yourself, family, and friends.

Happy cooking!

More Bestselling Titles from Dylanna Press

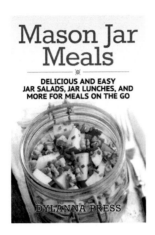

Mason Jar Meals by Dylanna Press

Mason jar meals are a fun and practical way to take your meals on the go. Mason jars are an easy way to prepare individual servings, so whether you're cooking for one, two, or a whole crowd, these fun, make-ahead meals will work.

Includes More than 50 Recipes and Full-Color Photos

In this book, you'll find a wide variety of recipes including all kinds of salads, as well as hot meal ideas such as mini chicken pot pies and lasagna in a jar. Also included are mouth-watering desserts such as strawberry shortcake, apple pie, and s'mores.

The recipes are easy to prepare and don't require any special cooking skills. So what are you waiting for? Grab your Mason jars and start preparing these gorgeous and tasty dishes!

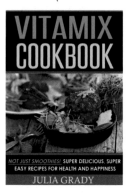

Vitamix Cookbook: Not Just Smoothies! Super Delicious, Super Easy Blender Recipes for Health and Happines by Julia Grady

Make the most of your Vitamix!

Whether your new to the world of high-speed blenders or have been using a Vitamix for years, the *Vitamix Cookbook: Not Just Smoothies! Super Delicious, Super Easy Recipes for Health and Happiness* is going to help you make amazingly healthy and delicious soups, dips, sauces, smoothies, desserts, and more.

Many people are excited when they first purchase a Vitamix but aren't really sure what to do with it besides make smoothies. While the Vitamix is great for making smoothies it has the potential to be used for so much more.

This book contains a plethora of recipes that can all be made quickly and easily right in your Vitamix. So what are you waiting for?

Healthy and Delicious Vitamix Recipes Including:

Nuts Milks
Nut Butters
Blender Burgers
Super Soups
Delicious Dips and Dressings
Sensational Sauces
Superfood Smoothies
Frozen Concoctions
...And More!
Get your copy today!
Happy blending!

The Inflammation Diet by Dylanna Press

Beat Pain, Slow Aging, and Reduce Risk of Heart Disease with the Inflammation Diet

Inflammation has been called the "silent killer" and it has been linked to a wide variety of illnesses including heart disease, arthritis, diabetes, chronic pain, auto-immune disorders, and cancer.

Often, the root of chronic inflammation is in the foods we eat.

The Inflammation Diet: Complete Guide to Beating Pain and Inflammation will show you how, by making simple changes to your diet, you can greatly reduce inflammation in your body and reduce your symptoms and lower your risk of chronic disease.

The book includes a complete plan for eliminating inflammation and implementing an anti-inflammatory diet:

• Overview of inflammation and the body's immune response – what can trigger it and why chronic inflammation is harmful
• The link between diet and inflammation
• Inflammatory foods to avoid
• Anti-inflammatory foods to add to your diet to beat pain and inflammation
• Over 50 delicious inflammation diet recipes
• A 14-day meal plan

Take charge of your health and implement the inflammation diet to lose weight, slow the aging process, eliminate chronic pain, and reduce the likelihood and symptoms of chronic disease.

Learn how to heal your body from within through diet.

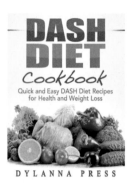

DASH Diet Slow Cooker Recipes by Dylanna Press

Delicious and Healthy DASH Diet Recipes for Your Slow Cooker

The DASH diet has once again been named the healthiest diet by top nutrition experts and there's no better time to start reaping the rewards of this smart, sensible eating plan. Eating the DASH diet way does not have to be boring, in fact, it contains the most delicious foods around – lean meats, whole grains, lots of fresh fruits and vegetables, and flavorful herbs and spices. So whether you are just starting out on the DASH diet or have been eating low-sodium for years, the *DASH Diet Slow Cooker Recipes: Easy, Delicious, and Healthy Recipes* is going to help you make delicious, healthy meals without spending a lot of time in the kitchen.

For this book, we've collected the best slow cooker recipes and adapted them to the DASH diet to create mouthwatering, family-pleasing dishes that can all be prepared easily and then cooked in your slow cooker while you're off doing other things. There's really nothing better than coming home at the end of a hectic day to the smell of tonight's dinner already prepared and waiting to be eaten.

These recipes feature fresh, whole foods and include a wide variety of recipes to appeal to every taste from classic dishes to new twists that just may become your new favorites. In addition, each recipe has less than 500 mg of sodium per serving, many a lot less than that.

In addition to recipes, the book includes a brief overview of the DASH diet as well as tips on how to get the most out of your slow cooker.

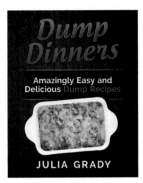

Dump Dinners: Amazingly Easy and Delicious Dump Recipes by Julia Grady

With the hectic pace of today's lifestyles getting dinner on the table every night is no easy task. When pressed for time, dump dinners make the perfect solution to the question, What's for dinner?

Dump dinners are so popular because they are so easy to make.

These recipes feature simple ingredients that you probably already have on hand in your freezer, refrigerator, and pantry. They do not require complicated cooking techniques or that you stand over the stove, stirring and sautéing. The majority of the recipes are mixed right in the pan they are cooked in, with the added bonus of saving cleanup time.

Delicious, Quick Recipes Your Family Will Love

This book contains the best dump dinner recipes around. None of these recipes take more than 15 minutes of hands-on time to prepare, and most a lot less. When you're short on time, you can turn to any one of these delicious recipes and have a home-cooked meal on the table with little effort and big rewards.
The recipes in this book can be cooked in several ways:
- Baked in the oven
- Cooked in a slow cooker
- Cooked on the stovetop
- Microwaved
- Frozen and cooked later

So whether you'd like to throw something in the slow cooker and come home hours later to an aromatic meal or pop a quickly prepared casserole into the oven, you are sure to find a recipe you and your family will love.

Index

138

70441365R00080

Made in the USA
San Bernardino, CA
01 March 2018